Tasty food
fussy kids

To my children, Nicholas, Lara and Scarlett

ANNABEL KARMEL'S FAVOURITES

Tasty food for fussy kids

Great recipes to tempt your picky eater

annabel karmel

1 3 5 7 9 10 8 6 4 2

Text copyright © Annabel Karmel 1999, 2006, 2007, 2011, 2013
Photographs copyright © Dave King 2006, 2011, 2013,
except page 20 Daniel Pangbourne 1999 and page 92 Ebury Press 2007
This edition copyright © Eddison Sadd Editions 2013

The Random House Group Limited Reg. No. 954009

A CIP catalogue record for this book is available from the British Library

ISBN: 978-009-195580-9

Printed in Hong Kong

Eddison•Sadd Editions
CREATIVE DIRECTOR Nick Eddison   INDEXER Dorothy Frame
SENIOR EDITOR Katie Golsby   DESIGNER Brazzle Atkins
PROOFREADER Nikky Twyman   ILLUSTRATIONS Nadine Wikenden
PRODUCTION Sarah Rooney

COVER PHOTOGRAPHY Dave King

Notes on the text:
- For fan-assisted ovens, reduce the temperature by 20°C.
- All black pepper is freshly ground.

Contents

Introduction

It's so easy to feel frustrated and powerless when your child simply refuses to eat certain foods. The majority of mums feel this way, and may equally feel that they are alone; that every child other than their own eats well. I felt that way – I wrote my first book because my son was a very fussy eater. However, around ninety per cent of children go through at least one lengthy phase of fussy eating.

While it can be frustrating when a child rejects the food we give them, their eating habits are hugely impacted by the way we deal with the situation. Eating habits and tastes are formed from an early age, so it's very important to try to get a good variety of foods into your child's diet from the outset. This not only helps with fussiness, but also ensures that they get all the nutrients they need for their development and long-term health.

Positive vibes

One of the most important things is to try and make mealtimes a fun, positive experience. Hide any frustrations you might have, and give your child lots of praise when she eats well or tries something new. This may mean that you have to ignore some of her bad behaviour.

Hide that frustration; food is one of the few things that children can control, so if your child can see that kicking up a fuss about food gets a rise out of you or, even better, a sweet treat, she'll carry on behaving in this way. It's amazing how quickly they can work this out.

Try new things

Try to keep your child's diet varied. Work out a menu at the beginning of the week; this will not only save time and money, but will also allow you to plan a delicious variety of meals that the whole family can enjoy. You can make certain evenings special by introducing food from around the world; have a look through this book for ideas. You will be surprised by the flavours that children enjoy, such as teriyaki (*see pages 45 and 65*) or barbecue (*see page 54*) sauces.

Recipe information

Each recipe is accompanied by helpful information on preparation and cooking times, how many portions the recipe makes and whether it's suitable for freezing. Preparation times and portion quantities should be used as a guide only, as these will vary.

Reward good eating

A lot of parents use reward systems to encourage their children to do chores, eat well or general good behaviour. They can be really effective when it comes to combating fussy eating. For younger children, try using a sticker chart: give a sticker for trying something new or for finishing a plate of food. Reward a completed chart with a treat; this should be something small and affordable – *not* an unhealthy food. Try to make it reasonably easy to attain a treat, so that your child doesn't lose interest. This will help to teach young children the purpose of these charts.

Slightly older children could be given an empty jar to fill with something like dried pasta: each time they finish their meal or try something new, they get a pasta shape to put in their jar. Once the jar is full, a small present or treat can be given as a reward.

Timing

The end of the school day is a great time to get children to eat something healthy, as they generally come home starving. The trouble is that most children will dive into the biscuit tin or grab a chocolate bar. Have something ready for your child on the table, to catch his eye before he gets as far as the biscuit tin. A plate of prepared fruit is more tempting than fruit in a fruit bowl, and most children like raw vegetables with a tasty dip. Delicious wraps, pitta pockets and pasta salads can be made quickly and easily, and it's a good idea to have a low shelf in the fridge where children can help themselves to tasty, healthy snacks.

Kids in the kitchen

Most children love getting involved in the kitchen; not only is there the magic of combining ingredients to create something new, but also the bond of sharing time and learning new things together. Teaching your child to cook can teach her invaluable skills, and encourage her to become interested in food. Why not invite a group of friends over and get them to prepare their own meal (younger children will need some supervision). Children are more likely to eat and be enthusiastic about something they have helped to make. Why not organize a cooking party? Choose a selection of recipes that the kids can make, such as pizza faces, fun cupcakes or biscuit shapes.

Eating together

Whenever possible, get the whole family eating together. This can really make a difference where fussy eaters are concerned. Take the time to have a relaxing chat, rather than focusing heavily on what is on the plates. This will help to take the pressure off children who may feel that what – and how much – they eat is being scrutinized.

With our modern, busy lifestyles, we all benefit a great deal from a sit-down meal with loved ones, taking time over our food, rather than wolfing down a quick bite in front of the television. This is important for good digestion and our enjoyment of food, not to mention family bonds.

Looks good enough to eat

Making things look appealing is just as important for kids as it is for adults. Looking and thinking about food is one of the first – and, some would argue, the most important – stages of digestion. Just thinking about food gets the juices flowing, and this literally means stimulating digestive juices and enzymes that help us to digest our food.

If food looks attractive and fun, children are far more likely to want to eat it. Giving individual portions helps make food more appetizing, and can make a meal seem less daunting. Mini versions of classics, like shepherd's pie, baked in small dishes such as ramekins, are always popular. This is a great way to cook a large quantity, as you can freeze single portions for use at a moment's notice.

Children also like to assemble their own food. Lay out a variety of ingredients for your child to put together. This works well with wraps or pizzas, and, whereas whole fruit may be ignored, thread bite-size pieces on to a skewer or straw and you're on to a winner. Making food preparation interactive in this way enhances the experience.

Healthy junk food

If your child loves burgers, nuggets and chips, get him to help you to make your own junk food. Try making pizzas with tortillas or muffins as the bases, or burgers using good-quality lean mince. Make chicken nuggets by marinating some chicken and coating it in breadcrumbs or crushed cornflakes or Rice Krispies. And how about making ice lollies from fresh fruit and pure fruit juice?

There are lots of ways to get your fussy eater interested in food. Hopefully, the recipes that follow will help. Remember: you're not alone. Keep trying, and good luck!

Vegetables

Winter parsnip and sweet potato soup

Melt the butter in a large saucepan. Add the onion and fry for 4–5 minutes. Add the parsnip and sweet potato and stir, then pour over the stock. Bring to the boil, then simmer for 15 minutes, until the vegetables are tender.

Whiz with an electric hand blender until smooth. Then add the cream and season to taste.

🔪 10 MINUTES
📺 25 MINUTES
🎨 4 PORTIONS
❄️ SUITABLE FOR FREEZING

a knob of butter
1 onion, peeled and sliced
1 medium parsnip (100 g/
  3½ oz), peeled and chopped
1 small sweet potato (300 g/
  11 oz), peeled and chopped
600 ml (1 pint) chicken or
  vegetable stock
2–3 tablespoons single
  cream (optional)
salt and pepper

Scrambled-egg tortilla wrap

✏️ 5 MINUTES

🍳 5 MINUTES

🍪 1–2 PORTIONS

❄️ NOT SUITABLE FOR FREEZING

1 large flour tortilla
a knob of butter
2 eggs, beaten
1 tablespoon milk
1 tablespoon chopped chives
1 tomato, deseeded and
  diced
25 g (1 oz) Cheddar cheese,
  grated
salt and pepper

Warm the tortilla in the microwave for 30 seconds on High. This will make it more pliable.

Melt the butter in a small frying pan. Beat the egg and milk together, then pour into the pan. Stir until scrambled, then add the chives, tomato and cheese, and season to taste.

Spoon the scrambled egg along one side of the wrap. Roll up to make a tube and slice in half.

Hidden-vegetable tomato sauce

⟋ 10 MINUTES

▭ 50–55 MINUTES

🍳 4 PORTIONS

❄ SUITABLE FOR FREEZING

Heat the oil in a saucepan and cook the onion over a low heat for 7–8 minutes. Add the garlic and cook for 1 minute. Add the carrot, courgette, butternut squash and mushrooms and cook for 4 minutes, stirring occasionally.

Add the balsamic vinegar and cook for 1 minute. Add the passata, tomato paste, sugar, stock, dried oregano, bay leaf and basil (if using). Cook, uncovered, over a low heat for 35–40 minutes.

Remove the bay leaf and blitz using an electric hand blender until smooth. Season to taste.

This is a great way to get children to eat vegetables. There are six vegetables blended into this tomato sauce, and what they can't see, they can't pick out. You could use sweet potato instead of butternut squash.

2 tablespoons light olive oil
1 medium onion, peeled and finely chopped
1 garlic clove, crushed
50 g (2 oz) carrot, peeled and grated
50 g (2 oz) courgette, topped and tailed and grated
50 g (2 oz) butternut squash, peeled, deseeded and grated
50 g (2 oz) button mushrooms, sliced
1 tablespoon balsamic vinegar
500 g (1 lb 2 oz) passata
2 tablespoons tomato paste
1 teaspoon soft brown sugar
200 ml (7 fl oz) vegetable stock
½ teaspoon dried oregano
1 bay leaf
a handful of torn basil leaves (optional)
salt and pepper

Courgette and tomato lasagne

⟋ 15 MINUTES

▦ 55–60 MINUTES

🍪 6 PORTIONS

✳ SUITABLE FOR FREEZING

1 tablespoon olive oil
1 red onion, peeled and
    chopped
2 garlic cloves, crushed
2 large courgettes, chopped
400 g (14 oz) tinned
    chopped tomatoes
1 teaspoon sugar
2 tablespoons tomato purée
1 teaspoon dried oregano
5 sun-dried tomatoes,
    chopped
a few drops of Worcestershire
    sauce
salt and pepper
6 sheets lasagne
150 g (5 oz) Gruyère cheese,
    grated

Cheese sauce
30 g (1 oz) butter
30 g (1 oz) flour
450 ml (¾ pint) milk
1 teaspoon Dijon mustard
50 g (2 oz) Parmesan cheese,
    grated

Preheat the oven to 220°C/430°F/Gas 7. Heat the oil in a saucepan, add the onion and fry for 3 minutes. Add the garlic and courgettes and fry for 8 minutes, until nearly soft. Add the tinned tomatoes, sugar, tomato purée, oregano, sun-dried tomatoes and Worcestershire sauce, bring to the boil, then cover and simmer for 5 minutes. Season to taste.

Meanwhile, make the cheese sauce. Melt the butter in a saucepan, then add the flour and blend in the milk, mustard and a little salt and pepper. Stir until thickened and smooth. Add the Parmesan and stir.

Arrange one third of the courgette and tomato sauce in the base of an ovenproof dish. Put 2 sheets of lasagne on top, then one third of the cheese sauce. Sprinkle over one third of the Gruyère cheese. Repeat twice so you have 3 layers, finishing with the Gruyère.

Put the lasagne in the oven and bake for 35–40 minutes, until it's cooked and the top is golden and bubbling.

Spotted snake pizza

⏱ 1 HOUR, 30 MINUTES

🎛 15 MINUTES

🍪 5 PORTIONS

❄ NOT SUITABLE FOR FREEZING

Put the yeast, water and sugar in a bowl and mix with a fork. Let the yeast dissolve and start to foam (about 10 minutes). Stir in the oil. Combine the flour and salt and add half to the bowl with a wooden spoon. Gradually add 150 g (5 oz) more flour, stirring until the dough leaves the sides.

Sprinkle some of the flour on to a work surface, then gradually knead in the remaining flour until the dough is no longer sticky (8–10 minutes). Place in an oiled bowl, cover with a damp tea towel and leave in a warm place for 50 minutes, or until doubled in size. Punch the dough down and put on a floured work surface. Knead until nice and elastic.

Preheat the oven to 200°C/400°F/Gas 6 and grease a large baking sheet. Divide the dough into about 18 balls, plus 1 larger ball for the head and a small piece for the tail. Stuff a Cheddar cube into the centre of each ball. Place them on the baking sheet in the shape of a snake, just touching. Brush the tops with the egg and cook for 10 minutes, or until lightly golden and joined together. Put tomato sauce and Mozzarella slices on to alternate balls, then top with pepper. Bake for 5 minutes. Add the olives for eyes and the green pepper for the tongue.

15 g (½ oz) active dried yeast
250 ml (8 fl oz) lukewarm water
a pinch of sugar
2 tablespoons olive oil
400 g (14 oz) strong white flour
1 teaspoon salt
75 g (3 oz) Cheddar cheese, cut into small cubes
1 egg, lightly beaten

Topping
10 tablespoons ready-made tomato sauce with herbs
200 g (7 oz) Mozzarella cheese, cut into slices
red, orange and yellow mini peppers, cored, deseeded and cut into small shapes
2 small black olives, stoned
1 small piece of green pepper, cut into a forked-tongue shape

Summer risotto

🖊 10 MINUTES

▭ 30 MINUTES

☕ 4–6 PORTIONS

❄ SUITABLE FOR FREEZING

900 ml (1½ pints) vegetable or chicken stock
1 tablespoon olive oil
40 g (1½ oz) butter
4 large shallots or 1 onion, peeled and finely chopped
1 garlic clove, crushed
50 g (2 oz) red pepper, deseeded and chopped
200 g (7 oz) Arborio rice
75 g (3 oz) courgette, diced
2 medium tomatoes (about 225 g/8 oz), skinned (*see box, right*), deseeded and chopped
4 tablespoons white wine
40 g (1½ oz) Parmesan cheese, grated
salt and pepper

Bring the stock to the boil and allow to simmer. Heat the oil and butter in a large frying pan and sauté the shallots (or onion) and garlic for 1 minute. Add the pepper and cook for 5 minutes, stirring occasionally, until softened. Add the rice, stirring for 1 minute to make sure it's well coated.

Add 1 or 2 ladlefuls of hot stock and simmer, stirring, until it's been absorbed, then add another ladleful of stock. Carry on doing this, stirring frequently. Then, after 10 minutes, add the diced courgette and tomato. Continue to add stock, then after about 8 minutes add the white wine. When all the stock has been added and the rice is cooked (this will probably take about 20 minutes), stir in the Parmesan cheese and season to taste.

To remove the skin from a tomato, cut a cross in the base using a sharp knife. Put in a bowl and cover with boiling water. Leave for 1 minute. Drain and rinse in cold water. The skin should peel off easily.

Vegetable burgers

Chop the pecan nuts in a food processor until finely chopped.

Put the sweet potato and carrot into a saucepan. Cover with water and bring to the boil, then simmer for about 15 minutes, until soft. Drain and mash.

Meanwhile, heat 1 tablespoon of the oil. Add the onion and squash and fry for about 8 minutes, until soft. Add the garlic and fry for 30 seconds.

Mix together all the ingredients except the flour and remaining oil. Shape the mixture into 8 burgers and coat in a little flour. Heat the oil in a frying pan and fry the burgers for 3 minutes on each side, or until lightly golden.

/ 20 MINUTES

▦ 30 MINUTES

🍪 8 BURGERS

✳ SUITABLE FOR FREEZING

50 g (2 oz) pecan nuts
150 g (5 oz) sweet potato, peeled and cut into chunks
2 medium carrots, peeled and chopped
2 tablespoons sunflower oil
1 onion, peeled and chopped
150 g (5 oz) butternut squash, peeled, deseeded and grated
1 garlic clove, crushed
60 g (2 oz) white breadcrumbs
50 g (2 oz) Cheddar cheese, grated
50 g (2 oz) Parmesan cheese, grated
2 teaspoons chopped thyme
salt and pepper, to taste
flour, for coating

Baked potatoes

/ 5 MINUTES

⬚ 60 MINUTES

◔ 1 PORTION

✳ SUITABLE FOR FREEZING
(WITHOUT FILLINGS)

1 medium baking potato
1 tablespoon milk
salt and pepper

Fillings

Spring onion and cheese
25 g (1 oz) Cheddar cheese,
   grated
1 tablespoon mayonnaise
2 spring onions, sliced

Baked beans and cheese
2 tablespoons baked beans
25 g (1 oz) Cheddar cheese,
   grated

Pesto and tomato
2 tablespoons pesto
15 g (½ oz) Cheddar cheese,
   grated
1 tomato, deseeded and
   chopped

Ham and cheese
25 g (1 oz) Cheddar cheese,
   grated
1 slice ham, chopped

Preheat the oven to 220°C/430°F/Gas 7. Scrub
the potato and prick it several times with a fork.
Bake for 45 minutes, or until the flesh is soft.
Alternatively, you could cook the potato in
the microwave for about 10 minutes.

Leave the potato to cool a little, then cut in
half and scoop out the flesh, leaving a layer of
potato on the skin.

Preheat the grill to High. Mash the potato with
the milk, then mix in your chosen filling. Season
and spoon back into the skins and place on a
baking sheet. Pop under the grill for 5 minutes,
until bubbling and golden.

*Potatoes contain vitamin C and are a good source
of potassium.*

Fish

/ 15 MINUTES

▦ 20 MINUTES

◷ 2 PORTIONS

✳ NOT SUITABLE FOR FREEZING

2 tablespoons freshly
  squeezed orange juice
1½ tablespoons clear honey
2 teaspoons dark soy sauce
150 g (5 oz) skinless salmon
  fillet (2 cm/¾ in thick, so
  not tail end)
2 bamboo skewers, soaked
  in water for 30 minutes

Noodles

70 g (2½ oz) medium egg
  noodles or ready-to-use
  fine thread noodles
½ teaspoon sesame oil
1 teaspoon sunflower oil
a handful of mangetout, cut
  into matchsticks
¼ red or orange pepper, cut
  into thin strips
2 spring onions, sliced
a handful of beansprouts
2 tablespoons water
1 tablespoon dark soy sauce
1 tablespoon sesame seeds,
  lightly toasted

Salmon on a stick with stir-fried noodles

Put the orange juice, honey and soy sauce in a small saucepan. Bring to the boil and cook for 1 minute, or until slightly thickened. Leave to cool.

Preheat the grill to High. Halve the salmon lengthways and thread on to 2 skewers. Fold over any thin belly pieces so that the fish is an even thickness. Place on a foil-lined grill tray, brush on some sauce and grill for 2 minutes. Coat with more sauce and grill for 1 minute. Turn over and repeat.

If the salmon is very thick, baste the sides with the juices from the pan and grill for 1 minute on each side. Reserve any left-over sauce. Keep the salmon warm while you cook the noodles.

Cook the noodles (if necessary) according to the packet instructions, then drain and toss in the sesame oil.

Heat the sunflower oil in a wok and stir-fry the mangetout, pepper and spring onion for 2–3 minutes. Add the beansprouts and the noodles, and cook for 1½–2 minutes. Toss in the left-over cooking liquid from the salmon with the water, soy sauce and sesame seeds.

Fish Balls

Heat the butter and oil in a saucepan and sauté the onion for about 3 minutes, then add the carrot and cook until the onion is lightly golden. Put all the ingredients in a large bowl and mix well. Shape the mixture into 20 walnut-size balls.

Fry the balls carefully until golden brown all over and the fish is cooked through. Drain on kitchen paper.

15 MINUTES
20 MINUTES
20 BALLS
SUITABLE FOR FREEZING

25 g (1 oz) butter
a little sunflower oil, plus extra for frying
1 onion, peeled and finely chopped
1 small carrot, peeled and finely grated
450 g (1 lb) mixed fish fillet (cod, haddock, bream, hake or whiting), skinned and chopped
1 egg, beaten
2 dessertspoons sugar
salt and pepper, to taste

Salmon fishcakes

Boil the unpeeled potato in salted water for 25–30 minutes, until tender (test with a table knife). Drain and, when cool enough to handle, peel and mash.

Put the salmon in a microwave-proof dish with the lemon juice and butter, and cook on High for about 2 minutes, until you can flake the fish with a fork. Alternatively, put the fish in a saucepan with the fish stock, bring to the boil and poach for a couple of minutes, then strain. Flake the salmon on to a plate and leave to cool slightly.

Mix the potato with the spring onions, chilli sauce, tomato ketchup, mayonnaise and seasoning. Fold in the flaked salmon, taking care not to break up the fish too much. Take 1 tablespoonful of the mixture and form into a small cake. Repeat with the remaining mixture, then dust with the seasoned flour.

Heat the oil in a non-stick pan and fry the fishcakes for 2–3 minutes on each side, until golden.

🖊 10 MINUTES
🖳 40 MINUTES
🍪 8 SMALL FISHCAKES
❄ NOT SUITABLE FOR FREEZING

1 medium potato
70 g (2½ oz) salmon fillet, skinned
a squeeze of lemon juice (for microwave method)
a knob of butter (for microwave method)
150 ml (¼ pint) fish stock (for poaching)
2 spring onions, chopped
1 teaspoon sweet chilli sauce
2 tablespoons tomato ketchup
½ tablespoon mayonnaise
salt and pepper, to taste
1 tablespoon seasoned flour, for dusting
2 tablespoons sunflower oil, for frying

Sweet and sour fish

🔪 10 MINUTES

⌗ 10 MINUTES

🍳 2 PORTIONS

❄ SUITABLE FOR FREEZING

200 g (7 oz) cod fillets,
  skinned and cut into
  cubes, or sole fillets,
  skinned and cut into strips
plain flour, seasoned with
  salt and pepper
1½ tablespoons vegetable oil

Sweet and sour sauce
100 ml (3½ fl oz) fish stock
  (use half a stock cube)
1 tablespoon white wine
  vinegar
1 tablespoon caster sugar
1½ tablespoons tomato
  ketchup
½ tablespoon soy sauce
½ tablespoon cornflour
3 tablespoons water
½ teaspoon sesame oil
1 tablespoon finely sliced
  spring onion

Coat the fish in the seasoned flour. Heat the
vegetable oil in a frying pan and sauté the fish
for 3–4 minutes or until cooked (it should flake
easily with a fork).

Mix the sauce ingredients and heat gently in a
saucepan, stirring until thickened. Pour the sauce
over the fish, heat through and serve on a bed of
fluffy white rice.

*This sauce is worth a try if you are having difficulty
getting your child to eat fish, as it will mask any
strong fishy taste. This recipe would also work using
chicken breasts cut into cubes, and chicken stock
instead of fish stock.*

Drunken fish
with little trees

First, make the sauce. Mix the cornflour with a little cold stock in a saucepan. Blend in the remaining stock, soy sauce, oil, sugar and rice wine vinegar. Stir over the heat until thickened, then add the spring onions.

Steam the broccoli florets for about 5 minutes, until just tender.

Toss the fish in the seasoned flour. Heat the oil and butter in a frying pan, then add the sole and fry for 1½–2 minutes. Flip the fish, pour over half of the sauce and remove from the heat. Toss the broccoli in the remaining sauce, heat through and serve.

Giving food fun names can encourage children to eat – for instance, 'little trees' is a good way to describe broccoli florets.

🖊 10 MINUTES

📟 15 MINUTES

Ⓖ 4 PORTIONS

✳ SUITABLE FOR FREEZING

100 g (3½ oz) broccoli, cut into florets
4 lemon sole fillets, skinned and cut into thick strips
30 g (1 oz) plain flour, seasoned with salt
1½ tablespoons sunflower oil
a knob of butter

Sauce
1 tablespoon cornflour
250 ml (8 fl oz) chicken stock
2 teaspoons soy sauce
1 teaspoon sesame oil
1 tablespoon caster sugar
1 teaspoon rice wine vinegar
2 spring onions, sliced

Golden fish fingers

🔪 15 MINUTES

🍳 5 MINUTES

🍽 2 PORTIONS

❄ NOT SUITABLE FOR FREEZING

30 g (1 oz) cornflakes
200 g (7 oz) cod fillets,
    skinned (or use sole or
    plaice)
salt and pepper, to season
20 g (¾ oz) plain flour
1 egg, lightly beaten
1½ tablespoons sunflower
    oil

Tartare sauce
150 ml (¼ pint) mayonnaise
lemon juice, to taste
1 tablespoon chopped
    parsley
1 tablespoon chopped
    capers
2 teaspoons chopped
    gherkins
1 tablespoon chopped chives

Put the cornflakes in a plastic bag and crush with
a rolling pin, then spread them out on a plate.

Cut the fish into 6 strips and season. Coat
with the flour, then dip in the egg and coat with
the crushed cornflakes.

Heat the oil in a frying pan and sauté the
fish for 3–4 minutes, or until golden and cooked
through, turning halfway through.

To make the tartare sauce, simply mix together
all the ingredients. Serve with the fish fingers.

*Crushed cornflakes make a delicious coating for
fish fingers. If you like, you could add a pinch of
cayenne pepper.*

Mini fish pies

Preheat the oven to 200°C/400°F/Gas 6. Put the carrots into a saucepan and cover with cold water. Bring to the boil, cover and simmer for 5 minutes, then add the potatoes and simmer for about 15 minutes, until tender.

Meanwhile, start the filling. Melt the butter in a saucepan, then add the onion and fry until soft. Add the sugar, stir for 30 seconds, then add the flour and blend in the white wine vinegar and milk. Stir until thickened and smooth. Add the Parmesan, herbs and fish. Allow to simmer for 2 minutes, then spoon into 4 ramekins.

Drain the carrots and potatoes, then mash together with a knob of butter and 2 tablespoons of milk. Spoon the mash over the fish and run a fork over the top. Bake for 15 minutes, until bubbling and golden.

🖊 15 MINUTES

🍳 40 MINUTES

🎂 4 MINI PIES

❄ SUITABLE FOR FREEZING

1 medium carrot (100 g/ 3½ oz), peeled and chopped
400 g (14 oz) potatoes, peeled and cut into chunks
25 g (1 oz) butter, plus extra for the topping
1 onion, peeled and chopped
1 teaspoon caster sugar
2 tablespoons plain flour
2 teaspoons white wine vinegar
300 ml (½ pint) milk, plus 2 tablespoons for the topping
40 g (1½ oz) Parmesan cheese, grated
1 tablespoon chopped chives
1 teaspoon chopped dill
150 g (5 oz) cod fillets, skinned and cut into chunks
150 g (5 oz) salmon, skinned and cut into chunks

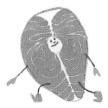

Annabel's paella

🔪 10 MINUTES

🍳 25 MINUTES

🍽 4 PORTIONS

❄ SUITABLE FOR FREEZING

200 g (7 oz) long grain rice
1 tablespoon olive oil
1 onion, peeled and chopped
1 garlic clove, crushed
1 teaspoon Spanish smoked
   paprika
½ red pepper, deseeded and
   chopped
200 g (7 oz) tinned chopped
   tomatoes
650 ml (23 fl oz) chicken
   stock
1 tablespoon tomato purée
170 g (6 oz) chicken, cooked
170 g (6 oz) prawns, cooked
55 g (2 oz) frozen peas
a handful of parsley,
   chopped (optional)

Put the rice in a colander and rinse well under cold running water. Leave to drain.

Heat the oil in a large non-stick frying pan or wok, and sauté the onion for 5 minutes, until soft. Add the garlic, paprika, pepper and rice and cook for 3 minutes, stirring constantly. Pour in the tinned tomatoes, stock and tomato purée. Simmer for about 15 minutes, until the rice is tender and the stock has been absorbed.

While the rice is cooking, shred the chicken into small pieces. Stir the chicken, prawns and peas into the paella, then cook for a further 2 minutes, until everything is heated through. Scatter over the parsley, if using.

It's important to use Spanish smoked paprika for this dish. It's available in supermarkets.

Chicken

Chicken and vegetable burgers

Preheat the oven to 180°C/350°F/Gas 4. Heat the oil and sauté the onion and leek for 3 minutes. Add the garlic and sauté for 30 seconds, then add the sage and sauté for 1 more minute. Mix together with all the remaining ingredients and shape into 12 burgers.

Heat some oil in a large frying pan and sauté the burgers for about 2 minutes on each side, until browned.

Transfer the chicken burgers to a baking sheet lined with baking paper and cook in the oven for 10–12 minutes, or until cooked through.

✎ 20 MINUTES

▭ 25 MINUTES

🍽 12 BURGERS

❄ SUITABLE FOR FREEZING

1½ tablespoons sunflower oil, plus extra for frying
1 onion, peeled and chopped
100 g (3½ oz) leek, chopped
1 garlic clove, crushed
6 sage leaves, chopped
100 g (3½ oz) fresh breadcrumbs
1 courgette (175 g/6 oz), topped and tailed, and grated
1 Pink Lady apple, peeled, cored and grated
1 large egg yolk
1 chicken stock cube, crumbled
500 g (1 lb 2 oz) minced chicken (breast and thigh)
salt and pepper

The dark meat from a chicken, such as the thighs, contains twice as much iron and zinc as the light meat.

Char-grilled chicken wraps

🔪 10 MINUTES

🍳 20 MINUTES

🍽 4 WRAPS

❄ NOT SUITABLE FOR FREEZING

4 large flour tortillas
2 tablespoons olive oil
2 chicken breasts, sliced
    into strips
3 teaspoons honey
salt and pepper
1 red onion, peeled and
    chopped
1 garlic clove, crushed
½–1 teaspoon cumin
1 tablespoon soy sauce
3 tablespoons tinned
    sweetcorn
150 ml (¼ pint) passata
75 g (3 oz) Cheddar cheese,
    grated

Warm the tortillas in the microwave for 20 seconds.
Heat 1 tablespoon of oil in a frying pan. Toss the
chicken in 2 teaspoons of the honey, then season.
Fry until browned and just cooked. Set the chicken
aside.

Heat the remaining oil and fry the onion for
4–5 minutes, until softened, then add the garlic
and cumin. Return the chicken to the pan, pour
over the soy sauce and 1 teaspoon of honey, then
add the sweetcorn and some salt and pepper.

Preheat the grill to High. Divide the filling
between the tortillas and roll up. Place on a
greased baking sheet, pour over the passata
and sprinkle with cheese. Grill for 5 minutes,
or until the cheese is bubbling and golden.

*Garlic can help fight infection, as it has both
antibacterial and antiviral properties.*

Chicken and gravy casserole

🔪 10 MINUTES

🍳 25 MINUTES

🍽 3 PORTIONS

❄ SUITABLE FOR FREEZING

2 chicken breast fillets, cut
    into strips
salt and pepper
2 teaspoons olive oil
2 onions, peeled and thinly
    sliced
1 teaspoon finely chopped
    thyme
a pinch of brown sugar
1 teaspoon balsamic vinegar
300 ml (½ pint) beef stock
½ teaspoon Worcestershire
    sauce
¼ teaspoon tomato purée
2 level teaspoons cornflour
a little cold water

Season the chicken, then heat the oil in a deep
frying pan and cook the chicken on both sides
until lightly golden. Transfer to a plate and set
aside.

Add the onions to the pan and sprinkle over
the thyme. Cover and simmer over a low heat for
8–10 minutes, until the onions are very soft. Add
the sugar and balsamic vinegar and fry until
lightly golden. Add the stock, Worcestershire
sauce and tomato purée and bring to the boil.
Blend the cornflour with the water, then add to
the pan, stirring until the gravy has thickened.

Return the chicken to the pan. Cover and
simmer over a low heat for 4–5 minutes, until
cooked through. Serve with mashed potatoes.

Teriyaki chicken skewers

Mix all the marinade ingredients together and marinate the chicken for at least 30 minutes.

Preheat the grill to High. Thread the chicken on to the skewers and grill for 4–5 minutes on each side, or until the chicken is cooked through.

🔪 10 MINUTES, PLUS 30 MINUTES FOR MARINATING

🍳 20 MINUTES

🍴 4 SKEWERS

❄ NOT SUITABLE FOR FREEZING

2 large chicken breast or thigh fillets, each cut into 4 strips
4 bamboo skewers, soaked in water for 30 minutes

Marinade
1 garlic clove, crushed
a small piece of ginger (about 1 cm/⅓ in), peeled and grated
2 tablespoons soy sauce
1 teaspoon sesame oil
3 teaspoons runny honey
1 tablespoon rice wine vinegar

Annabel's chicken dippers

Mix together the cheeses, breadcrumbs, paprika, cayenne pepper and seasoning, and place in a shallow dish. Put the beaten egg in another dish and the flour in a third. Dip each chicken strip first in the flour, then in the egg, and finally coat in the breadcrumb mixture.

Pour the oil into a frying pan over a medium heat. Fry the chicken dippers in batches, taking care not to overfill the pan, and sauté for about 2 minutes on each side until golden and cooked through. Then drain on absorbent kitchen paper.

✎ 15 MINUTES

▭ 10 MINUTES

🍽 4 PORTIONS

❋ SUITABLE FOR FREEZING
(BEFORE FRYING)

20 g (³/₄ oz) Parmesan cheese, grated
20 g (³/₄ oz) Cheddar cheese, grated
4 tablespoons dried breadcrumbs
¹/₂ teaspoon paprika
¹/₄–¹/₂ teaspoon cayenne pepper
salt and pepper
1 egg, lightly beaten
2 tablespoons flour
2 chicken breasts (about 250 g/9 oz), cut into 1 cm (¹/₃ in) strips
6 tablespoons sunflower oil

These are good served with tomato ketchup or tartare sauce.

Chicken pasta bake

/ 3 MINUTES

☐ 15–20 MINUTES

🕒 4 PORTIONS

❄ SUITABLE FOR FREEZING

125 g (4½ oz) pasta shells
1 tablespoon olive oil
1 onion, peeled and chopped
1 garlic clove, crushed
1 large chicken breast fillet,
  sliced
1 teaspoon balsamic vinegar
400 g (14 oz) tinned
  chopped tomatoes
1 tablespoon sun-dried
  tomato paste
3 tablespoons tinned
  sweetcorn
2 tablespoons chopped basil
1 teaspoon caster sugar
75 g (3 oz) Cheddar cheese,
  grated

Cook the pasta, following the packet instructions, then drain.

Heat the oil and fry the onion until softened. Add the garlic, chicken and balsamic vinegar and fry for 1 minute. Add the tinned tomatoes, sun-dried tomato paste, sweetcorn, basil and sugar. Simmer for 3 minutes, until the chicken is cooked.

Preheat the grill to High. Spoon the mixture into an ovenproof dish and sprinkle with the cheese. Pop under the grill for 5 minutes, until bubbling.

Chicken contains the antioxidant selenium, which helps to protect us from heart disease and some cancers.

15 MINUTES

▭ 30 MINUTES

◔ 4–6 PORTIONS

✺ SUITABLE FOR FREEZING

2 tablespoons oil
1 onion, peeled and chopped
75 g (3 oz) white breadcrumbs
350 g (12 oz) minced or
    chopped chicken (mix of
    breast and thigh)
50 ml (2 fl oz) milk
50 g (2 oz) Parmesan cheese,
    grated
½ teaspoon dried oregano
1 egg white
salt and pepper
a little flour

Tomato sauce
800 g (28 oz) tinned
    chopped tomatoes
2 tablespoons tomato purée
a pinch of sugar
1 small garlic clove, crushed
2 tablespoons chopped basil
    (optional)
250 g (9 oz) spaghetti

Chicken balls in tomato sauce with spaghetti

First make the chicken balls. Heat 1 tablespoon of oil in a frying pan, add the onion and fry until soft, then set aside to cool. Put all the ingredients into a food processor, except the flour. Whiz until finely chopped, then divide the mixture into 24 balls and roll them in the flour.

Heat the remaining oil in the frying pan. Add the chicken balls and fry until golden and cooked through.

To make the sauce, combine the tinned tomatoes, tomato purée, sugar, garlic and basil (if using). Add to the pan with the chicken balls, and simmer for 15 minutes.

Cook the spaghetti according to the packet instructions, drain, and serve with the chicken balls and tomato sauce.

Chicken contains much less fat than other meats, as most of the fat lies in the skin, which can be removed.

Chicken Bolognese

Heat the oil in a large saucepan. Sauté the onion, pepper, carrot and celery (if using) for 8–10 minutes, until softened. Add the garlic and thyme and cook for 1 minute. Add the chicken, turn up the heat a little, then cook for 2–4 minutes, stirring constantly, until the chicken has coloured slightly. Add the remaining ingredients, except seasoning. Bring to the boil, then reduce the heat and simmer for 20–30 minutes, until thickened. Season to taste and serve with pasta.

🥄 10 MINUTES

🗓 35–50 MINUTES

🍪 4–6 PORTIONS

❄ SUITABLE FOR FREEZING

1 tablespoon olive oil
1 onion, peeled and finely chopped
¼ red pepper, deseeded and diced
1 small carrot (60 g/2 oz), peeled and chopped
½ small stick celery, chopped (optional)
1 garlic clove, crushed
¼ teaspoon chopped thyme
250 g (9 oz) minced chicken
400 g (14 oz) tinned chopped tomatoes
150 ml (¼ pint) chicken stock
2 tablespoons tomato purée
1 tablespoon sun-dried tomato purée or tomato ketchup
1½ teaspoons sugar
salt and pepper

If your child has a tendency to pick out vegetables, cook the vegetables until they are soft, add the tomatoes and blend until smooth. Brown the chicken in a separate frying pan, then add the blended vegetables along with the remaining ingredients, and simmer as described above.

Chinese chicken and rice

Cook the rice following the packet instructions, adding the peas 4 minutes before the end of the cooking time. Drain well.

Meanwhile, heat the oil in a frying pan, add the onion and fry for 3 minutes. Add the pepper and garlic and fry for another 5 minutes, until softened. Add the chicken and fry until just cooked, then add the rice, peas and sweetcorn.

Mix together all the sauce ingredients, pour over the chicken and rice and fry for 1 minute.

Mix the salt into the eggs. Heat the oil in a frying pan, pour in the eggs and tip the pan so that the egg covers the base to make a thin omelette. Cook for 2–3 minutes, until just set. Turn out on to a board and cut into thin strips. Add to the rice and serve.

It has long been recognized that garlic lowers the risk of heart disesase and stroke through its effect on blood-clotting mechanisms.

🖉 10 MINUTES

▨ 20 MINUTES

☕ 4 PORTIONS

❋ SUITABLE FOR FREEZING

175 g (6 oz) long grain rice
50 g (2 oz) frozen peas
1 tablespoon olive oil
140 g (5 oz) onion, peeled and finely chopped
80 g (3 oz) red pepper, deseeded and diced
1 teaspoon garlic purée
150 g (5 oz) chicken breast fillet, diced
50 g (2 oz) tinned sweetcorn
2 eggs, lightly beaten
a pinch of salt
1½ teaspoons sunflower oil

Sauce
2 teaspoons hoisin sauce
1 teaspoon ketchup
2 teaspoons soy sauce
1 teaspoon honey
100 ml (3½ ml) chicken stock

Chicken in barbecue sauce

/ 10 MINUTES

25 MINUTES

3 PORTIONS

SUITABLE FOR FREEZING

1 carrot, peeled, cut in half
   lengthways, then sliced
2 tablespoons sunflower oil
1 onion, peeled and chopped
1 garlic clove, peeled and
   chopped
300 ml (½ pint) chicken stock
3 tablespoons tomato
   ketchup
1½ tablespoons soy sauce
1 tablespoon brown sugar
2 teaspoons Worcestershire
   sauce
½ teaspoon balsamic vinegar
2 teaspoons cornflour
1 tablespoon cold water
2 chicken breast fillets, diced
salt and pepper

Cook the carrot in boiling water for 5 minutes,
then drain. Alternatively, steam it for 5 minutes.

Heat 1 tablespoon of the oil in a saucepan.
Add the onion and fry until tender. Add the garlic
and fry for another 30 seconds. Add the stock,
ketchup, soy sauce, sugar, Worcestershire sauce
and balsamic vinegar. Mix the cornflour with the
water and add to the sauce. Stir until thickened.

Heat the remaining oil in a frying pan and fry
the chicken until browned. Add to the sauce with
the carrots, bring to the boil, reduce the heat and
simmer for 5 minutes. Season to taste and serve
with rice.

Potato and chicken rösti

🔪 15 MINUTES

🍳 15 MINUTES

🍴 4 PORTIONS

❄️ NOT SUITABLE FOR FREEZING

200 g (7 oz) potato, peeled
  and grated
6 spring onions, sliced
75 g (3 oz) chicken breast
  fillet, cooked and diced
50 g (2 oz) frozen peas
25 g (1 oz) Parmesan cheese,
  grated
1 large egg, beaten
1 tablespoon flour
salt and pepper
2 tablespoons vegetable oil
a knob of butter

Wrap the grated potato in a clean teatowel, and squeeze out the liquid. Put the remaining ingredients in a mixing bowl, season well and combine.

Heat 1 tablespoon of the oil and the butter in a frying pan with a diameter of 20 cm (8 in). Add the mixture and press it flat. Cook for 5 minutes, until lightly golden, then slide it on to a plate. Heat another tablespoon of oil in the pan, turn over the rösti and return it to the pan for about 7 minutes, until cooked through.

Meat

Swedish meatballs

20 MINUTES

25 MINUTES

4–6 PORTIONS

SUITABLE FOR FREEZING

Preheat the oven to 200°C/400°F/Gas 6. Line a baking sheet with non-stick paper.

Heat the oil in a saucepan, add the onion and fry for 5 minutes, until soft. Add the garlic and fry for another 30 seconds. Allow to cool.

Put all the meatball ingredients into a bowl and combine. Shape into 24 balls and place on the baking sheet. Put them in the oven for 15 minutes, until browned and cooked through.

To make the sauce, heat the oil in a saucepan, add the onion and fry for 5 minutes. Add the flour, then blend in the stock and cream. Add the remaining ingredients, bring to the boil, then simmer for 5 minutes. Add the meatballs and coat in the sauce. These are good served with pasta.

1 tablespoon olive oil
1 onion, peeled and chopped
1 garlic clove, crushed
100 g (3½ oz) breadcrumbs
30 g (1 oz) Parmesan cheese, grated
1 egg yolk
2 teaspoons chopped thyme
150 g (5 oz) minced pork or chicken
200 g (7 oz) minced beef
salt and pepper

Sauce

1 tablespoon olive oil
1 onion, peeled and chopped
2 tablespoons plain flour
400 ml (14 fl oz) beef stock
100 ml (3½ fl oz) double cream
2 teaspoons soy sauce
1 tablespoon Worcestershire sauce
½ teaspoon Dijon mustard
1 teaspoon chopped thyme
1 teaspoon sugar

Sweet and sour meatballs

✎ 25 MINUTES

▭ 35 MINUTES

☻ 5 PORTIONS

✾ SUITABLE FOR FREEZING

450 g (1 lb) lean minced beef
1 onion, peeled and chopped
1 apple, peeled, cored and
    grated
50 g (2 oz) fresh white
    breadcrumbs
1 tablespoon chopped parsley
1 chicken stock cube, finely
    crumbled
2 tablespoons cold water
salt and pepper
2 tablespoons vegetable oil

Sweet and sour sauce
1 tablespoon soy sauce
½ tablespoon cornflour
1 tablespoon vegetable oil
1 onion, peeled and chopped
50 g (2 oz) red pepper,
    deseeded and chopped
400 g (14 oz) tinned
    chopped tomatoes
1 tablespoon malt vinegar
4 tablespoons pineapple juice
1 teaspoon brown sugar
green pepper, deseeded and
    finely sliced (optional)

Mix together all the ingredients for the meatballs, except the oil, and chop for a few seconds in a food processor. Using floured hands, form the mixture into about 20 meatballs.

Heat the oil in a frying pan and sauté the meatballs, turning occasionally, until browned and sealed (10–12 minutes).

Meanwhile, make the sauce. In a small bowl, mix together the soy sauce and cornflour. Heat the oil in a pan and sauté the onion for 3 minutes. Add the red pepper and sauté, stirring occasionally, for 2 minutes. Add the tomatoes, vinegar, pineapple juice and sugar, season with pepper and simmer for 10 minutes. Add the soy sauce mixture and cook for 2 minutes, stirring occasionally.

Blend and sieve the sauce, or purée through a mouli. Pour the sauce over the meatballs, cover and simmer for about 5 minutes, or until cooked through. Serve with basmati rice and garnish with green pepper, if liked.

Mini meatloaves

Preheat the oven to 200°C/400°F/Gas 6. Lightly grease 12 cups in a mini-muffin tray or 6 cups in a standard muffin tray.

Heat the olive oil and sauté the onion for 5 minutes, then stir in the thyme. Remove from the heat and leave to cool slightly.

Meanwhile, put the bread in a food processor and whiz into crumbs. Add all the remaining ingredients, including the sautéed onion (but not the tomato sauce), and whiz for 1–2 minutes, until combined.

For mini meatloaves, put 1 tablespoonful of the mixture into each cup of the prepared tray and bake for 15 minutes. For larger meatloaves, allow 2 tablespoonfuls of mixture and bake for 20 minutes.

Remove from the trays with a spatula and serve with the tomato sauce.

To freeze, put the meatloaves on a baking sheet lined with clingfilm. Cover with more clingfilm and freeze until solid. When frozen, transfer to a freezer bag. Defrost overnight in the fridge or for 1–2 hours at room temperature. You can reheat in the microwave or oven.

✏ 10 MINUTES

⬜ 15–20 MINUTES

🍳 12 MINI MEATLOAVES

❄ SUITABLE FOR FREEZING

½ tablespoon olive oil, plus extra for greasing
½ onion, peeled and finely chopped
½ teaspoon chopped thyme
2 slices white bread, crusts removed
250 g (9 oz) lean minced beef
3 tablespoons tomato ketchup
1 teaspoon Worcestershire sauce
4 tablespoons milk
½ teaspoon salt
freshly ground black pepper
1 quantity Hidden-vegetable tomato sauce (*see page 17*) or your favourite tomato sauce

Lamb Koftas

✏️ 10 MINUTES

🗔 12–15 MINUTES

🍳 8 SKEWERS

❄️ SUITABLE FOR FREEZING

50 g (2 oz) breadcrumbs
1 onion, peeled and finely
   chopped
250 g (9 oz) minced lamb
2 tablespoons chopped mint
1 garlic clove, crushed
1 egg yolk
¼ teaspoon cinnamon
½ teaspoon ground
   coriander
1 teaspoon soy sauce
salt and pepper
8 bamboo skewers, soaked
   in water for 30 minutes

Preheat the oven to 220°C/430°F/Gas 7. Grease a baking sheet with oil.

Combine all the ingredients in a bowl, then shape into 16 balls. Thread two balls on to each skewer.

Place the skewers on the prepared baking sheet and cook for 12–15 minutes, until golden and cooked through.

Iron is the most common nutritional deficiency in young children, often leading to tiredness and a lack of concentration. Meat provides the best source of iron, and ensuring that your child gets enough can markedly improve their academic performance.

Teriyaki beef skewers

Put all the sauce ingredients into a small saucepan and whisk until smooth, then bring to the boil and simmer until thickened slightly. Pour into a ramekin, reserving 1 tablespoon of the sauce.

Slice the steak into 12 strips about 6 cm (2¼ in) long. Thread on to the skewers. Pour over the reserved sauce, and season.

Heat a little oil in a frying pan. Fry the skewers for 1 minute on each side, then leave to rest for 3 minutes. Serve with the dipping sauce.

🔪 15 MINUTES

🍳 10 MINUTES

🍽 3 PORTIONS

❄ NOT SUITABLE FOR FREEZING

200 g (7 oz) thin sirloin steak
salt and pepper
a little sunflower oil, for frying

Sauce
2 tablespoons rice wine vinegar
1½ tablespoons soy sauce
2 tablespoons dark brown sugar
1 teaspoon sesame oil
1 teaspoon cornflour
12 bamboo skewers, soaked in water for 20 minutes

Beef stir-fry

⟋ 10 MINUTES

▦ 20 MINUTES

☕ 4 PORTIONS

✳ NOT SUITABLE FOR FREEZING

2 carrots, peeled and thinly
  sliced
150 g (5 oz) broccoli, cut into
  florets
2 tablespoons sunflower oil
300 g (11 oz) sirloin steak,
  sliced into strips
salt and pepper
1 onion, peeled and sliced
1 garlic clove, crushed
100 g (3½ oz) beansprouts

Sauce
1 tablespoon cornflour
2 tablespoons hoisin sauce
2 tablespoons mirin
2 tablespoons soy sauce
1 tablespoon water

Bring a saucepan of water to the boil, add the
carrots and boil for 3 minutes. Add the broccoli
and boil for another 2 minutes, then drain.

Meanwhile, heat 1 tablespoon of the oil in a
frying pan. Season the steak, add to the pan, then
quickly brown and set aside.

Mix together the sauce ingredients. Heat the
remaining oil in the frying pan, add the onion
and fry for 3 minutes. Add the garlic, then the
carrots and broccoli and the steak. Pour over the
sauce and toss over the heat for 2–3 minutes. Add
the beansprouts, stir, then remove from the heat.
Serve with rice.

*Red meat is packed full of high-quality protein
as well as being the best source of easily absorbed
iron. It is also a good source of zinc and vitamin B12.*

Marina's tempting twirls

 10 MINUTES

🔲 40 MINUTES

🍴 4 PORTIONS

❄ SAUCE SUITABLE FOR FREEZING

250 g (9 oz) fusilli pasta
2 tablespoons olive oil
1 onion, peeled and finely chopped
1 garlic clove, crushed
½ red pepper, deseeded and finely chopped
250 g (9 oz) lean minced beef
1 tablespoon finely chopped flat-leaf parsley
1 teaspoon brown sugar
1 teaspoon Worcestershire sauce
1 tablespoon tomato purée
800 g (28 oz) tinned chopped tomatoes
1 beef stock cube, dissolved in 150 ml (¼ pint) boiling water
4 basil leaves, torn
salt and pepper

Cook the pasta, following the packet instructions, then drain and set aside.

Heat the oil in a large saucepan and sauté the onion for about 3 minutes, or until softened. Add the garlic, cook for 1 minute, then add the red pepper and cook for another 5 minutes, stirring occasionally.

Add the minced beef and cook for about 3 minutes, stirring occasionally, until browned. Add the parsley, brown sugar, Worcestershire sauce, tomato purée, tinned tomatoes and stock, bring to the boil, then simmer for 25 minutes. Add the basil leaves and season to taste.

Add the cooked pasta and toss with the sauce.

Pasta

Mummy's pot noodles

Cook the noodles according to the packet instructions (if necessary). Drain and set aside.

Put the stock, soy sauce, peas, sweetcorn and chicken in a saucepan over a medium heat. Bring to a simmer and cook for 2 minutes.

In a small cup, mix the cornflour with the water. Add to the pan and stir over the heat for 1 minute, until the liquid thickens slightly. Add the noodles and mix everything together. When the noodles are heated through, transfer to a bowl to serve.

 5 MINUTES

🍳 10 MINUTES

🍽 1 PORTION

❄ NOT SUITABLE FOR FREEZING

70 g (2½ oz) fine Chinese-style dried egg noodles or straight-to-wok fine thread noodles
125 ml (4 fl oz) chicken stock
1½ teaspoons dark soy sauce
25 g (1 oz) frozen peas
35 g (1¼ oz) drained tinned or frozen sweetcorn
50 g (2 oz) chicken, cooked and shredded
½ teaspoon cornflour
1 teaspoon cold water

These are always popular with kids, but the ones you can buy are really high in salt. It only takes a few minutes to make your own – it's fun to serve them in a cup.

Lara's lasagne

- ⟋ 15 MINUTES
- 🍳 50–60 MINUTES
- 🍽 6 PORTIONS
- ❄ SUITABLE FOR FREEZING

1 tablespoon olive oil
1 onion, peeled and chopped
1 garlic clove, crushed
½ red pepper, deseeded and chopped
450 g (1 lb) lean minced beef
½ teaspoon dried mixed herbs
400 g (14 oz) tinned chopped tomatoes, drained
295 g (11 oz) can condensed cream of tomato soup
salt and pepper

Cheese sauce
50 g (2 oz) butter
40 g (1½ oz) flour
460 ml (16 fl oz) milk
a generous pinch of ground nutmeg
50 g (2 oz) Gruyère cheese, grated
9 sheets fresh or dried lasagne
25 g (1 oz) Parmesan cheese, grated

Preheat the oven to 190°C/375°F/Gas 5. You will need an ovenproof dish 28 x 17 x 7 cm (11 x 6¾ x 2¾ in) in size.

Heat the oil in a large saucepan and sauté the onion, garlic and pepper until softened. Add the beef and herbs, and cook until the beef has browned. Add the tomatoes and soup and cook over a medium heat for 15–20 minutes. Season to taste.

Meanwhile, make the cheese sauce. Melt the butter in a small saucepan, then stir in the flour and cook for 1 minute. Gradually stir in the milk, bring to the boil and whisk until thick and smooth. Add the nutmeg and a little seasoning. Remove from the heat and stir in the Gruyère until melted.

Just cover the base of the dish with meat sauce, then cover with 3 sheets of lasagne. Spoon over half of the remaining meat sauce, then spoon over a little cheese sauce. Cover with 3 more lasagne sheets, then spoon over the remaining meat sauce. Spoon over a little more cheese sauce, then arrange the last 3 sheets of lasagne on top. Spread over the remaining cheese sauce, ensuring that the lasagne is well covered. Sprinkle over the Parmesan and put in the oven for 25–30 minutes.

Macaroni cheese with ham and peas

Cook the macaroni according to the packet instructions, adding the peas 4 minutes before the end of the cooking time. Drain.

Meanwhile, melt the butter in a large saucepan, then add the flour and whisk in the milk. Stir until thickened. Add the mustard and 100 g (3½ oz) of the Cheddar and stir until the cheese has melted. Add the pasta, peas, ham and seasoning.

Preheat the grill to High. Spoon the mixture into a shallow heatproof dish and sprinkle over the remaining Cheddar. Put under the grill for 5–8 minutes, until bubbling and golden.

✎ 5 MINUTES

▦ 15–20 MINUTES

🍳 4–6 PORTIONS

❄ SUITABLE FOR FREEZING

150 g (5 oz) macaroni
100 g (3½ oz) frozen peas
30 g (1 oz) butter
30 g (1 oz) flour
450 ml (¾ pint) milk
1 teaspoon Dijon mustard
150 g (5 oz) Cheddar cheese, grated
100 g (3½ oz) ham, chopped
salt and pepper

Cheese is a perfect food for children. It provides an excellent source of protein and calcium, important for strong bones and good teeth.

📅 1 HOUR

🍽 8 PORTIONS

❄️ SUITABLE FOR FREEZING

2 tablespoons olive oil
1 small onion, peeled and
   finely chopped
1 small leek, thinly sliced
½ stick celery, chopped
¼ small red pepper,
   deseeded and chopped
1 small carrot, peeled and
   grated
½ dessert apple, peeled,
   cored and grated
1 garlic clove, crushed
400 g (14 oz) tinned
   chopped tomatoes
450 g (1 lb) minced beef
4 tablespoons tomato purée
2 tablespoons tomato
   ketchup
250 ml (8 fl oz) beef stock
¼ teaspoon dried oregano
salt and pepper

Hidden-vegetable Bolognese

Heat the oil in a large frying pan and sauté the vegetables, apple and garlic for 10 minutes, until softened. Transfer to a blender and add the tinned tomatoes, then whiz until smooth.

Wipe out the frying pan with a sheet of kitchen paper, then add the mince and fry over a medium-high heat until browned, breaking up the mince with a wooden spoon. If your child likes a fine texture, you can transfer the browned mince to the food processor and whiz for a few seconds.

Add the tomato and vegetable sauce to the frying pan with the mince, and stir in the tomato purée, ketchup, stock and oregano. Bring to a simmer and cook for 40–45 minutes, until the sauce is thickened. Season to taste and serve with spaghetti.

Pasta with tomato and mascarpone sauce

🔪 5 MINUTES

📅 20 MINUTES

🍽 4 PORTIONS

❄ SUITABLE FOR FREEZING

200 g (7 oz) novelty pasta shapes
1 tablespoon olive oil
1 red onion, peeled and chopped
30 g (1 oz) carrot
30 g (1 oz) courgette
15 g (½ oz) celery
1 garlic clove, crushed
50 g (2 oz) button mushrooms
400 g (14 oz) passata
½ teaspoon sugar
2 tablespoons torn basil leaves (optional)
100 g (3½ oz) mascarpone cheese
salt and pepper

Cook the pasta, following the packet instructions, then drain.

Heat the oil in a saucepan and sauté the onion, carrot, courgette and celery for 5 minutes. Add the garlic and sauté for 1 minute. Add the mushrooms and sauté for 2 minutes. Stir in the passata and sugar, then cover and simmer for 10 minutes, stirring occasionally. Remove the pan from the heat, add the basil and blend in a food processor. Return to the pan and add the mascarpone cheese. Stir until melted and simmer for 1–2 minutes. Season to taste.

Toss the pasta with the sauce and serve.

Most children like pasta with tomato sauce, and this provides a good vehicle for sneaking other ingredients into their diet! The novelty-shaped pasta adds interest. This sauce is good with steamed white fish or poached chicken.

Penne with chorizo and tomato sauce

Cook the penne following the packet instructions, then drain.

Meanwhile, heat the oil in a saucepan, add the onion and fry for 5–8 minutes, until softened. Add the chorizo and garlic and fry until lightly golden. Add the paprika, then the tinned tomatoes, tomato purée and sugar. Simmer for 5 minutes.

Add the pasta to the sauce with the Parmesan cheese.

5 MINUTES

15 MINUTES

4 PORTIONS

SUITABLE FOR FREEZING

200 g (7 oz) penne
1 tablespoon olive oil
1 red onion, peeled and
   finely chopped
70 g (2½ oz) sliced chorizo,
   chopped
1 garlic clove, crushed
½ teaspoon Spanish smoked
   paprika
800 g (28 oz) tinned
   chopped tomatoes
1 tablespoon tomato purée
2 teaspoons sugar
50 g (2 oz) Parmesan cheese,
   grated

Marina's pasta with pesto and cherry tomatoes

 8 MINUTES

⊡ 12 MINUTES

☕ 4 PORTIONS

❄ SUITABLE FOR FREEZING

250 g (9 oz) fusilli
2 tablespoons light olive oil
100 g (3½ oz) onion, peeled
   and sliced
1 garlic clove, crushed
200 g (7 oz) chicken breast
   fillet, cut into strips
200 g (7 oz) cherry tomatoes
1 tablespoon soy sauce
1 tablespoon balsamic
   vinegar
3 tablespoons green pesto
salt and pepper
Parmesan cheese, grated,
   to serve

Cook the fusilli, following the packet instructions. Drain and set aside.

Heat the olive oil in a large frying pan or wok, then add the onion and sauté for 3 minutes, stirring occasionally. Add the garlic and cook for 1 minute, then add the chicken and stir-fry for 2 minutes. Add the cherry tomatoes and stir for another 2 minutes, then add the soy sauce, balsamic vinegar and pesto, and cook for 1 minute before adding the pasta. Season with a little salt and pepper, and continue to cook for another minute or until heated through.

Sprinkle over a little Parmesan cheese before serving.

Sweet treats

White-chocolate and marshmallow Rice Krispie squares

Line a fairly shallow 20 cm (8 in) square baking tin with non-stick paper.

Break the chocolate into pieces and put in a saucepan together with the butter and golden syrup. Melt over a low heat. Put the Rice Krispies in a large bowl and stir in the melted chocolate mixture. Fold in the mini marshmallows.

Spoon the mixture into the prepared tin and level the surface with a potato masher. Place in the fridge to set and cut into squares before serving.

/ 5 MINUTES

⬜ 5 MINUTES

🍪 9 SQUARES

❋ NOT SUITABLE FOR FREEZING

100 g (3½ oz) white chocolate

75 g (3 oz) unsalted butter, cut into pieces

75 g (3 oz) golden syrup

100 g (3½ oz) Rice Krispies

25 g (1 oz) mini marshmallows

These Rice Krispie squares are fun, and easy for children to make themselves.

Chocolate and raisin oatmeal cookies

✎ 15 MINUTES

🖪 12 MINUTES

🍪 24 COOKIES

❄ SUITABLE FOR FREEZING

110 g (4 oz) butter, softened
115 g (4 oz) dark brown sugar
1 egg
150 g (5 oz) porridge oats
75 g (3 oz) self-raising flour
75 g (3 oz) raisins
a pinch of salt
1 teaspoon vanilla extract
100 g (3½ oz) plain
   chocolate chips

Preheat the oven to 200°C/400°F/Gas 6. Line two large baking sheets with non-stick paper.

Cream the butter and sugar together until light and fluffy. Beat in the egg with a whisk. Add the remaining ingredients and mix well.

Shape the mixture into 24 balls and place on the prepared baking sheets, leaving plenty of space between the balls.

Bake for 12 minutes, until lightly golden, but still soft in the middle.

Raisins and oats make a good combination: the high sugar content of raisins provides a quick release of energy, while the oats provide sustained energy.

Brownies with toffee sauce

Preheat the oven to 200°C/400°F/Gas 6. Line a 30 x 23 cm (12 x 9 in) tin with non-stick paper.

Melt the chocolate and butter in a bowl set over a pan of simmering water. When the mixture is runny, combine with the sugar, eggs, flour and cocoa powder, and whisk until smooth. Stir in the white chocolate chunks, then pour the mixture into the prepared tin. Bake for 35–40 minutes, until well risen and firm to the touch. Cut into 24 squares.

To make the toffee sauce, melt the butter and sugar in a small saucepan. Reduce the heat and stir in the cream and vanilla essence.

Serve the brownies with the toffee sauce, and maybe some vanilla ice cream.

✎ 20 MINUTES

🖾 35–40 MINUTES

🍪 24 BROWNIES

❄ NOT SUITABLE FOR FREEZING

100 g (3½ oz) milk chocolate
100 g (3½ oz) plain chocolate
200 g (7 oz) butter
150 g (5 oz) caster sugar
4 eggs
50 g (2 oz) self-raising flour
30 g (1 oz) cocoa powder
50 g (2 oz) white chocolate, cut into chunks

Toffee sauce
50 g (2 oz) butter
50 g (2 oz) light brown sugar
200 ml (7 fl oz) double cream
½ teaspoon vanilla essence

Eating chocolate makes us feel good, as it triggers the release of serotonin and endorphins in the brain, which have an uplifting effect.

Dairy- and egg-free chocolate and raspberry cupcakes

 20 MINUTES

⬛ 18–20 MINUTES

🍽 10 CUPCAKES

❄ SUITABLE FOR FREEZING
(WITHOUT JAM OR ICING)

150 g (5 oz) plain flour
40 g (1½ oz) cocoa powder
1 teaspoon bicarbonate of
   soda
175 g (6 oz) caster sugar
50 ml (2 fl oz) sunflower oil
200 ml (7 fl oz) hot water
½ teaspoon white wine
   vinegar
1 teaspoon vanilla extract
a little raspberry jam

Icing
75 g (3 oz) dairy-free
   margarine
75 g (3 oz) icing sugar
20 g (¾ oz) cocoa powder

Preheat the oven to 180°C/350°F/Gas 4. Line a muffin tin with 10 cupcake cases.

Put all the cake ingredients (except the jam) into a bowl and whisk until smooth. Pour the mixture into the cases (you may find it helpful to transfer the mixture to a jug first).

Bake the cupcakes for 18–20 minutes, until well risen and springy. Leave to cool a little in the tin, then transfer to a cooling rack. Spread a little raspberry jam over the top.

To make the icing, beat together the margarine, icing sugar and cocoa, and spread over the jam. Pop the cupcakes in the fridge to set the icing.

Malted chocolate milkshake

Measure the Ovaltine and boiling water into a jug. Stir until the Ovaltine has dissolved. Add the milk and ice cream. Whiz until smooth, using an electric hand blender.

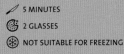 5 MINUTES

2 GLASSES

NOT SUITABLE FOR FREEZING

3 tablespoons Ovaltine
2 tablespoons boiling water
200 ml (7 fl oz) milk
200 g (7 oz) chocolate
  ice cream

Chocolate contains some ingredients that are good for you, such as iron, magnesium and calcium (in milk chocolate) – so don't feel too guilty about eating (or drinking) it.

Pancakes with caramelized apple

✎ 10 MINUTES

▦ 35 MINUTES

🍪 ABOUT 15 PANCAKES

❄ SUITABLE FOR FREEZING

225 g (8 oz) self-raising flour
1 teaspoon baking powder
2 eggs
50 g (2 oz) caster sugar
200 ml (7 fl oz) milk
sunflower oil, for frying
15 g (½ oz) butter
2 dessert apples, peeled,
  cored and sliced
1½ tablespoons brown sugar
maple syrup, to serve
  (optional)

Put the flour, baking powder, eggs, caster sugar and milk into a bowl, and whisk until smooth.

Pour a little oil into a frying pan to coat the base and, when hot, spoon enough batter into the pan to just cover the bottom. Fry for 1–2 minutes, then flip and cook the other side for 1 minute until golden. Repeat until you've used all the batter, using a little more oil each time.

Melt the butter in a small frying pan. Add the apples and fry for 2 minutes. Add the sugar, and stir until caramelized. Serve with the pancakes and a little maple syrup (if using).

To freeze, separate the pancakes with greaseproof paper.

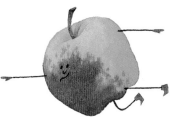

Caramel Bananas

Melt the butter in a frying pan with the sugar. Heat until the sugar dissolves and the butter is foaming. Add the bananas to the pan, stirring constantly for 2–3 minutes. Remove from the heat and add the orange juice.

Divide between 2 bowls and serve with toasted waffles and a scoop of vanilla ice cream.

🔪 3 MINUTES

🍳 20 MINUTES

🍪 2 PORTIONS

❄️ SUITABLE FOR FREEZING

15 g (½ oz) butter
25 g (1 oz) soft brown sugar
2 bananas, peeled and sliced
100 ml (3½ fl oz) freshly
   squeezed orange juice

Bananas are super versatile: they're great eaten alone as a snack, or included in smoothies, muffins or salads. They contain less water and more sugar than other soft fruits, which means they're a great energy provider. They're also packed with vitamin B6, which is needed for the production of red blood cells and for boosting the immune system.

Peach and strawberry jellies

⟋ 10 MINUTES, PLUS CHILLING

▦ 5 MINUTES

🍮 4 JELLIES

❄ NOT SUITABLE FOR FREEZING

5 gelatine leaves
200 ml (7 fl oz) raspberry
  and cranberry cordial
300 ml (½ pint) lemonade
100 g (3½ oz) strawberries,
  hulled and quartered
200 g (7 oz) tinned peach
  slices in syrup, cut into
  pieces

Soak the gelatine leaves in cold water for
5 minutes. Pour the cordial and lemonade into
a saucepan and heat until hand-hot. Remove the
pan from the heat. Squeeze the water out of the
gelatine, then add the leaves to the saucepan.
Stir until the gelatine has dissolved.

Divide the strawberries and peaches between
4 bowls or glasses. Pour over the jelly and leave
to set in the fridge for 6 hours, or overnight.

Strawberries contain more vitamin C than other
berry fruits: 100 g (3½ oz) provides almost twice
the recommended daily amount for adults.

Strawberry-sorbet ice lollies

🖊 7 MINUTES, PLUS FREEZING

🍪 4 PORTIONS

Put the sugar and water in a saucepan and boil until syrupy (about 3 minutes). Allow to cool.

Purée the strawberries using an electric hand blender, and combine with the cooled syrup and orange juice. Pour the mixture into the moulds and freeze until solid.

30 g (1 oz) caster sugar
40 ml (1½ fl oz) water
250 g (9 oz) strawberries, hulled and halved
juice of 1 medium orange (about 40 ml/1½ fl oz)
4 ice-lolly moulds

Tropical lollies

🖊 7 MINUTES, PLUS FREEZING

🍪 4 PORTIONS

Blend all the ingredients together until smooth. Pour into the moulds and freeze until solid.

Most manufactured lollies are full of additives, so why not make your own from fresh fruit?

To make two-tone lollies, half-fill the moulds with strawberry mix, freeze for about 2 hours, then fill to the top with tropical mix. Add the stick, and when frozen you'll have a red and orange lolly.

1 large mango, stoned, peeled and diced
180 ml (6½ fl oz) tropical fruit juice
3 tablespoons icing sugar
1 tablespoon freshly squeezed lemon juice
4 large ice-lolly moulds

Left: Strawberry-sorbet ice lollies

Index

About Annabel Karmel

Mother of three, Annabel Karmel MBE is the UK's number one parenting author and expert on devising delicious, nutritious meals for babies, toddlers and children.

Since launching with *The Complete Baby and Toddler Meal Planner* more than two decades ago, Annabel has written 37 books, which have sold over 4 million copies worldwide, covering every stage of a child's development.

With the sole aim of helping parents give their children the very best start in life, Annabel's tried-and-tested recipes have also grown into a successful supermarket food range. From delicious Organic Baby Purées to her best-selling healthy chilled meals, these offer the goodness of a home-cooked meal for those busy days.

Annabel was awarded an MBE in 2006, in the Queen's Birthday Honours, for her outstanding work in child nutrition. She also has menus in some of the largest leisure resorts in Britain and a successful app, *Annabel's Essential Guide to Feeding Your Baby and Toddler*.

For more information and recipes, visit **www.annabelkarmel.com**.

Acknowledgements

Louise Ward and Phil Carroll (Sainsbury's Books), Fiona MacIntyre, Martin Higgins and Cat Dowlett (Ebury), Dave King (photography), Tamsin Weston (props), Kate Bliman and Maud Eden (food stylists), Lucinda McCord (recipe testing), Nick Eddison and Katie Golsby (Eddison Sadd), and Sarah Smith (PR).

annabel karmel

Other titles in the series are:

ANNABEL KARMEL'S FAVOURITES

First foods
*Recipes and advice
to help you wean
your baby*

Suitable from four months

ANNABEL KARMEL'S FAVOURITES

Exploring
new tastes
*Introduce your baby
to new flavours
and textures*

Suitable from six to nine months

ANNABEL KARMEL'S FAVOURITES

Growing
independence
*Healthy home-made
recipes to encourage
self-feeding*

Suitable from nine
to twelve months

ANNABEL KARMEL'S FAVOURITES

Toddler
meals
*Nutritious recipes for
your child to enjoy
with the family*

Suitable from one year

ANNABEL KARMEL'S FAVOURITES

Lunchboxes
*Quick, easy and
healthy ideas to
make lunchtime fun*

50 healthy recipes

ANNABEL KARMEL'S FAVOURITES

Family
meals
*Quick and easy
recipes to keep
meal times fresh*

50 healthy recipes

ANNABEL KARMEL'S FAVOURITES

Vegetarian
meals
*Delicious, nutritious
recipes for veggie kids*

50 healthy recipes

ANNABEL KARMEL'S FAVOURITES

Party food
*Quick, quirky and
fun ideas for your
child's celebration*

50 healthy recipes

ANNABEL KARMEL'S FAVOURITES

Kids in the
Kitchen
*Creative recipe
ideas to make and
bake together*

50 healthy recipes